transVersing

Breakwater Books
P.O. Box 2188, St. John's, NL, Canada, A1C 6E6
www.breakwaterbooks.com

We acknowledge the support of the Canada Council for the Arts, which last year invested $153 million to bring the arts to Canadians throughout the country. We acknowledge the financial support of the Government of Canada and the Government of Newfoundland and Labrador through the Department of Tourism, Culture, Industry and Innovation for our publishing activities.

Printed and bound in Canada.

Breakwater Books is committed to choosing papers and materials for our books that help to protect our environment. To this end, this book is printed on a recycled paper that is certified by the Forest Stewardship Council®.

 Canada Council for the Arts   Conseil des Arts du Canada

 Newfoundland Labrador   Canadä

 FSC   MIX   Paper from responsible sources   FSC® C004071

TRANSVERSING

For the Love of Learning

CONTENTS

FOREWORD

In September 2016, as a transgender activist and the executive director of For the Love of Learning (FTLOL), a local St. John's charity that provides at-risk youth with arts-based training, I approached the wonderful playwright and actor Berni Stapleton and the equally amazing writer and actor Robert Chafe with the idea for a performance that would dramatize the issues transgender youth struggle with every day in our community. From those early connections, an incredible partnership formed between FTLOL and the creative minds at Artistic Fraud.

Submissions for this project were received from the youth at FTLOL, all of them strong first-person accounts and artistic reflections on life as a transgender person. These were powerful works of art expressing both the timeless human desire for understanding and the unending creative desire to break down the walls that separate us. From these potent primary sources, playwrights Berni Stapleton and Sharon King-Campbell crafted the magnificent dramatic text for *transVersing*, which weaves these compelling individual creations into a vibrant communal fabric filled with movement, emotion, and courage.

A cast was then formed by none other than our remarkable contributing writers: Violet Drake, Daze Jefferies, Fionn

Shea, Perin Squires, Taylor Stocks, and Dane Woodland. And *transVersing* made its theatrical debut on March 28, 2017, at the Barbara Barrett Theatre in St. John's.

Now, after numerous public performances, we are publishing *transVersing* for the first time with the help of Breakwater Books. Part one of this groundbreaking collection includes individual pieces from the original contributors, and part two presents the original dramatic text by Stapleton and King-Campbell.

Although transgender issues are finally on the forefront in our society, transgender people still experience discrimination on multiple levels. We hope that *transVersing*, both as a theatrical production and as a published book, will continue to raise public awareness and help to foster the egalitarian and imaginative power of empathy, which has always been the unspoken generator of true democracy and social justice.

Gemma Hickey
Executive Director,
For the Love of Learning
St. John's, NL

VIOLETDRAKE

Bookworm

in my youth
i found solace
within a book
more than anywhere

ink
never screamed
nor did paper
ever hit

stories
have always
fashioned and
fascinated me

be about masks, dummies, and vampires
or lions, witches, and wardrobes
pages bound together could always
be found between my palms

the book was my umbrella
during the storms of my peers,
a sanctuary only my eye could see
where my *I* was at peace

a place where
I/eye
could be
anywhere (else)

beyond the four walls
of brick and cement,
pristine and ivory:
matching the armour across my face

i'd watch the other boys
from here,
the pedestal
for all Other boys

all those who were outside
the main text;
one that we all learned
from the jersey room to sandy point

the same text
that left me illegible
to those
that birthed me

i wonder
what frankenstein's creature
would make of me
if i visited its shack?

would i be
adam? or eve?
or instead
another fallen angel?

where i come from
gender is thought to be
intransient; a dichotomous stone
mirroring the underbelly of this island

still,
i breathe
and weave
a *you and me*

i reside
on this rock
just as you
and the rest of us do

i too
have had my fair share
of tickets from the gender police,
and trips to manning's beach

when my school crest
changed from burgundy to blue,
i graduated from HNMA
yet never enrolled into manhood

my first winter
as a university student
had me read both fiction and fact;
through both i grew my voice

this marked the first time
that the word
transgender
welcomed me in school

it was in my very first dorm
where the same palms
that held the shield of my younger self
crafted me a key instead

the key to a place
far greater than the imaginary,
more dangerous than narnia,
and certainly more magical than hogwarts

it's 2012 and i'm in the backseat
of my parent's trusted minivan
where i disclose in between their screams:
i'm transgender

my mother replies:
you just think
you are the next thing
you read in your books

i can't help but wonder
how different
all this would be
if she too were a bookworm

GENDERSYNTHESIS

on the cusp of
adolescence
is when i found
virtue without virtus

september 8th, 2010:
otherwise known as
the anniversary of
myself and makeup

each time this month
sprouted on the calendar
i was greeted with
a ripe new grade

by the time that my
front lawn turned lush
the beauty bug had
already infected me

whereas most boys my
age spent their summer
fulfilling their father's hunting pacts,
i made my own with the mirror

they set snares
as i set powder,
both of us bonded
in execution

my trophy animal
found not in trees
but between selves:
the rhizome of envy

crisp lines of slate
across the eyelid,
or architecture of
an alabastrine complexion

detoxifying my eyes
i unearth myself,
becoming chimera:
hybrid, implausible, absurd

encased inside
four navy walls
is where i committed
my first murder

the amalgamation
of rigour and diligence;
a crime traced in
kohl and rouge

bade adieu to qualms
with each stroke
forging me anew;
facere vera

apostle androgyne
through osmosis is
heir to a new faith,
catharsis sans catholicism

i begin to grow akin
to the power of glass
reap what i sow
on uncharted terrain

bearing witness
to none but me
i make my initial molt,
the onset of my haunting

when my eyes met hers
for the very first time
a glimpse of home
was found to be mine

the imagined made real
shot adrenaline through
every stem of me:
gendersynthesis

visceral now victorious,
a new epistemology
is born situated
against the grain

drunk on pride,
my newfound wings
glide me down the hall
to my father's dwelling place

wide eyed and bright
i showcase the fruit
of my labour, to which he responds:
what have you got done to yourself my son?

the gloss in my eye dimmed
and toward the hall i ran,
flesh seared in scorn
and blood boiled in shame

magic mutated into monstrosity,
i crawl back into my cave
vowing never to let another
burn me for my beauty again.

GHOST GIRL

i wander around
this world every day
yet i go
completely unseen

my gender is
ectoplasm
just a trace left by
a phantom like me

what does it mean
to be a ghost
a being trapped between this world
and the afterlife

is there even a life
after one such as this:
a life of translucency,
indecency, and strife

my identity is often
transparent and lost;
at best dislocated,
dismembered, or disavowed

most think i am found in
the blackness that frames eyes
yet in the heart of every dead boy
is where i reside

eyes
lips
stares
and glares

caught between
distain and desire,
pass through me as if i am nothing
but nothingness itself

i am the air that is inhaled
during your gasps,
the carbon dioxide
released from your exhale

the glue that
keeps everything together:
taken for granted
and unseen

we are often deceived
by the sparkle of visibility
recognition fuels volition
a queer activist says to me

but how many women like me
have died chasing that rabbit
down the hole that leads her
to venus extravaganza's wonderland

a girl like me is not unusual
yet often made a spectacle,
who better to know
the high price of being a muse

to cross genders is carnivalesque:
suspension in transition,
truth mutated
into transgression

my trace is found
in the racing hearts
of women like me
walking home at night

the ways in which
our bodies
and genders
are defined and confined

policed and disposed of
for the threat of resisting order
i wish my sister leelah alcorn
could have grew older

my pulse is felt in every:
sorry, i'm just not used to this,
what exactly are you and *i didn't mean to be*
offensive, you know what i mean though

i'm bruised by all the:
i'm just not into that,
so really you are a man,
or *you'll find someone right for you someday*

always exhausted of the unfairness in:
but i'm the one who gave birth to you,
you've deceived me for so long,
and *then why bother doing this if it's this hard?*

constantly plagued by the uncertainty of:
am i going to come home tonight,
will i ever feel okay in the skin i am in,
or *who will ever love me if i tell the truth?*

who attains to me in my time of need
to soak my wounds
and nourish my soul
when my shoulders get weak

everyone in this city
is travelling in one way or another
but how many apparitions like me
are stuck in limbo

what creatures
of this island
are part of my clan
of vampires

can't find themselves
in the hanging glass,
left with stomachs
full of thorns

monsters that blend
vitality and fatality,
augment the organic
with the artificial

all craving a taste
for the same
invigorating blood:
an antidote for dysphoria

MADE TO LOVE

when i was 14
i found myself
on a sheet
of cold steel

my eyes drowned
in a sea of white
with nothing but my
heartbeat as the soundtrack

it all happened so fast
fear couldn't catch up
caught between life and death
i was about to erupt

dizzy from red and blue lights
the only relic of me
behind a mask of plastic
was the hope of my return

do people know
what it's like
to awaken from
an artificial sleep

finding yourself one with machine
missing a part on the inside
welcomed by many more on the outside
scattered across a foreign home

i know what quarantine feels like
every thought in your head
when your limbs are lead
and the unfamiliar greets you in the mirror

for me it was a cyborg
but for you—a stranger
someone devoid of all colour
tired and full of phlegm

i wish i was your visitor
have my eyes warm yours
remind you what lies beyond
hotel hospice

you could tell me if
the lion i fell for
ever comes out of the grey
jungle he has found himself in

would your arms
melt into mine
or would a frightened
little boy push me aside

do remember that i have cared
for a boy like him once before
my heart is no stranger
to those who push away instead of pull in

i want to stitch
yours back together
so i can witness and touch
all of where it's been broken

from you i've learned
to find fires in glaciers
work from the inside out
and not to swim against the current

that love is not enough
but hope is
and to never stop moving
for it's how all of us stay alive

i still have the scar from
where they took the poison out
it ran larger and deeper than expected
much like i for you

i need you to know
that every step of mine outside
is to nothing but your heartbeat
as my soundtrack

DAZEJEFFERIES

BLOWMEDOWN

only good
souvenirs
go on
display

over here

in nanny
and poppy's
place

we all
learn to:

      pull up
      spuds

           speak in
           tongues

                    stog the
                    stove

            with

      birch

junks

o,

my past
in those
rural
seasons

was
cruel –

dogberries
flung
at me

my butterfly net
snapped in half

by lawless
boys

with
missing
teeth

εϊ3

           εϊ3

                         εϊ3

had to learn
to be rough

and stop
wearing
good clothes

my jesus

this little heart
turned cold,

my home
too white,

and rusty
yet we didn't
want the dirt
inside

when it
filled our cuts

we'd make a poultice (never pronounced the T)
↓
careful
not to
burn
our
tongues

see,

tough's
not enough

when can
we talk

about
pleasure?

dionysus
under control

how two men
might find
themselves
caught up in
each other

♫ *at the village* ♫

the place
where self
and other
fool around

what a goings-on

never eroded into
island history

our remarkable YYT

i first
heard the word
transgender

when i was
fourteen

it was unanimous,

so ask me

again:

must be from away, is ya?

i've been here
the whole time
you didn't look

get your skin?

i smell it
burning

where's your woman?

inside me

it takes more
than two
or three
queer sticks
to keep the
fire going

CAME THROUGH

two
great circles
intersecting

float
me on

absorb
me into
the culture
of another

out on
the water

at first
blush

you touch it:

apocryphal
piece of me

tucked

between
pages

written in
german

*may i
ask a
personal
question?*

i don't
know

what it
feels like

down there

trudging
through
basements

of
flooded
homes

producing
an image

of
inimical
mercy

intercut with the
third movement
of your tongue

pool of spit

but,

*do you
like that?*

making the
male design

the home
of my own

leaves

cracks
in the
stoutest
bits

fucking
with my

terra cotta

the
gesso
dries

just
too
hard

you think
i'd learn
better

as an
architect

we want
to keep
things warm

filling the
open heart/h

with our
visibilities
aglow

and
lips
locked

fluids
spray

into
the
bow

all those
erosions—

no hands now

but the
wheel
turns
faster

won't
you

crash

and
slam
this
head

into

SRS
airbag

harder

how
does
that
feel?

this is our
expanding
phase

where we
learn to meet
each other's

demands

follow
through
with the
service—

i make
things
up in
my head

a story

about

miss fish

out of water

trying
to make
a living

with
no shells

so she
sells
herself

for
sand
dollars

gives up
on her
god-beliefs

doubles back for
undistinguished
objects ahead

all this
rumbles
out of me

and
the veil
looms
large

that
bitch

that
brain

ho/e
and
an axe

staring
back
through
dirty
glass—

one of
these days

i'm
gonna
beat it
all up

i know
that
things
shatter

if you
strike
them
hard
enough

in this
direction

i play

with
the gift

i am given

my saint,
my john

some
rough
looking

but he
came
through

sending
me flying

OTHERLOVERS

butterfly stuck in honey
won't you attack and release me?
don't you want my body?
let me give you jeopardy

give in and you'll see that
my body is a strong shield
but wrapped around me is
the tether you wield

can't cut the memories of
our little broken home
it's you who drowns me
and still i love you so

i told you years ago
i don't know how to sow
tiny seeds
i can't fill their needs
but i can make them grow
other lovers will go

it's a curse that i'm under
can't you feel the thunder?
gave you power before her
didn't i love you better?

FIONNSHEA

ITERATION #2

I am a bastard child of the American dream and American identity. I am a bastard child because I was born into a body that refuses to conform, a mind that refuses the binary, and a soul that refuses a black-and-white identity. I am a bastard child because I was born into a society that rejects my manhood, that forces my womanhood, and that knocks me down while telling me to pick myself up by the bootstraps. Because that's the American dream, right—work hard and you'll succeed?

Well I've worked hard. And damn if I won't succeed.

See, I am a bastard child in my identity, but also in my age. Like my country, I am young. And when we're young, we expend so much time and so much creative energy trying to change the things that people made fun of—"Your voice is too high, your stature is too small, but you're legitimate! You're just not enough."

I am a bastard child of America, but I've learned from those who have come before me: I've learned that our existences are not a mistake, that we are not invisible. This is something to shout from the rooftops when they send the dogs after us. It is something to sing in the streets even when we are blocked by white supremacists...and state legislators...it is something to be played in the theater, even when the crowds have all gone home, and it is the thing that unrelenting visibility, above all, that we must bring to light to save our lives and our communities from the trap of fear that is the unknown.

So, for the boy who cannot come out for fear his parents will disown him, for the girl who is told she in invisible in the school halls and the senate halls, I have one message: we hear you, we will hold your hands; we must stay together, no matter what our gender, no matter what our skin colour, no matter if we're born here (like you, like me) or immigrants (like me, like you). We've been down this road before, we, the young, the old, the strong, the hungry: we know hatred. We know bigotry. We know fear. We do not have the privilege of sitting quiet while our family dies, not when walking out your front door is an act of rebellion and every breath resonates like a gunshot—until we die or it changes, keep fighting.

I am a self-made American bastard. And I plan to stay that way.

POEM

You tight-lipped, silver-tongued, Goddess-worshiping,
    moonlight baby, snowfall huntress
You were born into blood and born to the bleeding
the cord wrapped thrice around your neck
the noose you wouldn't wear in life was formed by your
    life itself
Backwards, upside-down, crying, you came into the
    world screaming heathen rites,
blood boiling in the midwife's veins and she thought
    you a fairy child
blood ritual anointed your birth
your mother knew that soon you would begin to bleed
You strong, fierce, tender-hearted, sharp-minded hunter
You were built from pieces taken out of the body of your
    Mother
any gender can bleed
a learned skill from blood mother and blood father
Changeling-child, river-driver, quick-footed, wordsmith,
    dragon
The sac that once held you gave way to your own walls,
    the umbilical cord severed
but the link held fast
your blood still flows with the moon rites
boys can bleed too

ITERATION #1

Thou, Nature, art my goddess; to thy law
My services are bound. Wherefore should I
Stand in the plague of custom, and permit
The curiosity of nations to deprive me,
For that I am some twelve or fourteen moonshines
Lag of a brother? Why bastard? Wherefore base?
When my dimensions are as well compact,
My mind as generous, and my shape as true,
As honest madam's issue? Why brand they us
With base? with baseness? bastardy? base, base?
Who, in the lusty stealth of nature, take
More composition and fierce quality
Than doth within a dull, stale, tired bed
Go about creating a whole tribe of fops
Got b'tween sleep and wake
Well then, legitimate Edgar, I must have your land.
Our father's love is to the bastard Edmund
As to th' legitimate. Fine word- "legitimate"!
Well, my legitimate, if this letter speed,
And my invention thrive, Edmund the base
Shall top th' legitimate. I grow; I prosper.
Now, gods, stand up for bastards!

ITERATION #3

I came out as queer in the middle of Shakespeare's *As You Like It*. Not in your typical "I was backstage and I had a catharsis" kind of way—a kind of way that went more like: "Were it not better... That I did suit me all points like a man?"

I remember the way sweat dripped down my back as I stood in the spotlight, the way my scene partner turned to me and delivered her lines without an inch of comprehension. I remember going backstage and changing in the single-stall bathroom, even though the women's dressing room was next door. For the final scene, I grudgingly changed from a button-down into a dress, my Rosalind as uncomfortable as I was.

"Do I make you that squirmy?" Orlando teased.

It wasn't you, Orlando. It was never you.

Who am I? I'm a writer. I'm an actor. I'm a musician. I'm an adored brother. I'm a beloved daughter, my parents' little one. I'm a student. I hope to be a politician. And although it doesn't define me, I'm also transgender.

What does that mean? It means although I am beautiful my mirror hardly reflects who I am. It means I cannot use, for fear of vitriol or rape, the bathroom of my self-assigned gender identity. It means it would be better if bathroom doors were labelled "get yelled at" or "get beat up," and I often walk a half hour across campus to find a gender-neutral bathroom, or don't bother using the bathroom at all.

It means I am stared at when I walk down the street or order coffee. It means I have too short hair and too round hips and too high a voice and my drivers' license is marked with that F—fuck.

I am also young. And when we're young, we expend so much time and so much creative energy trying to hide who we really are, trying to change things that people made fun of—"your voice is too high, your stature is too small, but you're legitimate! You're just not enough."

My teenage self believed this self-defacing bullshit, but my teenage self had an outlet. My teenage self had theatre. My teenage self had Shakespeare. The Bard was an escape, a mirror that helped me understand my reality.

> I, that am not shaped for sportive tricks,
> Nor made to court an amorous looking-glass;
> I, that am rudely stamp'd, and want love's majesty
> To strut before a wanton ambling nymph;
> I, that am curtail'd of this fair proportion,
> Cheated of feature by dissembling nature,
> Deformed, unfinish'd, sent before my time
> Into this breathing world, scarce half made up,
> And that so lamely and unfashionable
> That dogs bark at me as I halt by them;
> Why, I, in this weak piping time of peace,
> Have no delight to pass away the time,
> Unless to spy my shadow in the sun
> And descant on mine own deformity
>
> *(Richard III* 1.1. 14-27)

I was drawn to Richard III because I knew what it was like to have society treat you as an illegitimate freak. I was drawn to Edmund in *King Lear*, because I knew what it was like to be seen as a bastard son.

I was expending creative energy not on trying to change myself, but trying to tell my story through the voice of a character. When I finally came out, it was Edmund's monologue that ran through my mind: "Now, gods, stand up for bastards!"

I dare you to look at my body and tell me I am deformed.

I dare you to look at me and tell me I don't exist.

I dare you to look at me and tell me I am not enough.

I dare you, because I can: I am a bastard child of America, just like Edmund, just like Rosalind, unseen, unheard, and if fighting back means being called a faggot bastard, so be it. I've learned from daring people to believe me: I've learned that my existence is not a mistake and that I am not deformed or unfinished. It is something to shout from the rooftops when they send the dogs after us, it is something to sing in the streets even when we are blocked by riot police, it is something to be played in the theater, even when the crowds have all gone home, it is the thing that we must bring to light to save our lives and our communities from the trap of fear that is the unknown—

Come hell, come high water, come April, I will pack my bags as Edmund did, and fly back to the United States of America. For the little boy who cannot come out for fear his parents will disown him, for the little girl who cannot use the correct bathroom, I have one message: we've got your back, rise up, we will hold your hand, rise up; we must stay together, no matter what our gender, no matter what our skin colour, no matter if we're born here (like you, like me) or immigrants (like me, like you). We've been down this road before, we, the young, the old, the strong, the hungry, the musicians, the actors: we know hatred. We know bigotry. We know fear. We do not have the privilege of sitting quiet while our family dies, not when walking out your front door is an act of rebellion and every breath resonates like a gunshot—until we die or it changes, keep fighting.

I am a self-made American bastard. And I plan to stay that way.

PERINBRADLEESQUIRES

ARMY CADETS

When I lived on the west coast of Newfoundland, I joined The Army...Cadets.

As much as I defy structures, expectations, and any sense of "logic," I really found comfort in knowing who I was, where I was expected to be, and knowing my place in the small world that was 2904 Cambrai Army Cadets. I loved the forced comradery, the adventure. The unflattering uniforms. The fact we all had to wear a hat, cover our hair. Pretend we were neutral, the same.

In Army Cadets I could blend in with the other kids, hide my developing sex, and pretend I was one of the guys.

During the summer of 2004 (grade seven) I had left my small town of Port au Port (twenty minutes outside of Stephenville, an hour away from the nearest Chapters, and eight and a half hours away from Costco) to go to Camp Argonaut, located in the army base of Gagetown, New Brunswick. I was so excited to leave Port au Port for the summer, to shed the stigma of being a cop's daughter that had haunted me from my first day of grade one, and finally make some friends. At this point in my life I knew I wasn't a girl. Or at least what others deemed to be a girl. I had already started taking control of my body by demanding only boy's clothes (unless I had to attend a formal event. No amount of tears and screaming could weasel me out of a dress then).

In Army Cadets, the only thing that separated the boys and the girls was hair. Boys had to have their hair off their necks, shorter than their ears. Girls had to have a neat and tight bun. Though I was the best shot in Cadets, I couldn't put my hair in a bun by myself to save my life. This is when I knew I had an out.

"Mom, I want to have short hair."

The first time I cut all of my blonde ringlets off, my mom cried. I don't think she knew exactly why she was so upset, but I did. And it made me feel alive. I looked in the mirror after having to convince the hairdresser that I didn't in fact want a pixie cut, and yes I knew I would look like a boy. I did look like a boy. I smiled. Mom cried. The hairdresser said it would grow back. I never let it.

I also have to mention that in 2015 when I moved to London, Ontario, and I was visiting my mom back in Port au Port, she gave me a little plastic bag in a box, and before I opened it she laughed, "I kept it."

"Kept what?"

"Your hair."

I threw it out as soon as I moved.

TAYLORSTOCKS

DEFINITIONS *(song)*

I don't know how to be a boy
To grow up and have man as my choice
To grow old with a baritone voice
I don't know how to be a boy

I don't know how to be a girl
To grow up and be a woman in the world
To grow old as my lady unfurls
I don't know how to be a girl

Now I gotta ask
What the hell do you know of that
From where I'm sitting
It's not as if you've got a good definition
Maybe it's true
I'm not so different from you
Well how about that

I don't know how to be man
To take up space cuz they all say I can
To hold the world in the palm of my hand
I don't know how to be a man

I don't know how to be a femme
To save myself from being consumed by men
To grow old and not take shit from them
I don't know how to be a femme

So you know I gotta ask
What the hell do you know of that
From where I'm sitting
It's not as if you've got a good definition
Maybe it's true
I'm not so different from you
Well how about that

I know how to be me
Turns out I don't mind my own company
When I'm myself, I am truly free
I know how to be me

TRANS LIFE ON THE ROCK *(song)*

My boyfriend, he left me yesterday
He told me, girl, you are too queer
I said I don't know what you're saying
There ain't no woman standing here.

      I'm a transient twister, an elegant mister
          A boy big sister with a cock
      My gender it flows cuz that's how it goes
          Living trans life out on the rock
        I sparkle and glow so all of you know
        I'm living trans life out on the rock

Woke up today feeling kind of lazy
I didn't want to have to werk it giiiiirl
Something in my head was driving me right crazy
Felt like it was me against the world
What do you do when your chest betrays you
Your best assets make you feel like a fool

      I'm a transient twister, an elegant mister
          A boy big sister with a cock
      My gender it flows cuz that's how it goes
          Living trans life out on the rock

I sparkle and glow so all of you know
I'm living trans life out on the rock

I want you to know that being she makes me feel queasy
I want you to know that the men of the world won't let
     me be he
I want you to know that the woman inside of me is still
     alive and
I want you know I want you to know...

I'm a transient twister, an elegant mister
A boy big sister with a cock
My gender it flows cuz that's how it goes
Living trans life out on the rock
I sparkle and glow so all of you know
I'm living trans life out on the rock

WOKE

Wouldn't it be nice
to wake up

                    the same person I was
                    when I went to sleep

INVITE ME

Invite me into your life
and I will twist myself into your definitions of beauty
Taking bliss through my contortions
Even as I'm bound

Invite me into your body
and I will mirror the wondrous heavens of your
     landscape
Making flesh come alive under fingertips
Even as I'm untouched

Invite me into your soul
and I will thread my heart through your eye
Stitching sovereignty within you
Even as I unravel

THE PROMISE CALL

They call for me
and I am pulled
toward

                          a safety
        enrobed in the trappings of smallness

They offer
                      a prize
for my complacency
                         praise
for their comfort

How could I resist the promise of such protection?

RAINBOWS

There are rainbows in my chest
swirling, in the cavern of my rib cage
Bright colours, though dark ones too
Ever changing,
constant movement
within a static frame.

And who doesn't want a heart full of rainbows?
The delightfulness of such simple coloured pleasure as
    an added topping upon daily drudgery –
it seems a gift to have such a spectacle so close to my
    lungs

For each one of my breaths is filled with rich hues
    vibrantly mixed with the next and next
until my throat is charged with multicoloured text
Words filled with wisdom of what it is to
move with a force of nature.

But,
Sometimes they make me sick
An oily gasoline sheen sticking between my ribs
Yet too slippery to grip
It makes me queasy

The shifting and lilting
my stomach can't keep up with the ragged rhythms
tossed about in a storm that can't decide if it is
        fundamentally more aligned with the inherent
        internal properties of red or blue

Philosophy is no life boat.

There are no answers,
few words that allow communication across the tempest
And sometimes it takes too much
To figure out what it takes to be seen
when alignment is a laughable construction.

There isn't, then,
Much else to be done
Except to move too
And enjoy the pretty colours as they come.

FIVE DAYS OF CREATION

Before I was born, I ran away.
     I had whispers of the wrong words, of what...I
     couldn't say.
When I saw a shadow of myself, I hid
in the promise of perfect-precious womanhood.

And I screamed when my gut said no!
Drowning out the doubt,
But I wouldn't be the same,
'Cause I couldn't quite escape
that perhaps I wanted out...

On day one, I heard a wilted echo.
Sitting 'round the circle, watching as the mouth bled,
Breathing every beat, feeding what I didn't know...

So I painted him and he came alive!
Standing in the mirror, looking at me through my eyes,
I couldn't feel my chest for the chafing of the tape, but,
Here he was of me, in him, for me to realize.

On the second day, I clung to the breeze,
Desperate for the company that comes from being she.
I swore I'd make room in those words;
It was never my intention to give them to the birds...

But I just couldn't find my verse.
Even up on stage, I was plagued by the girl curse –
Damning petty little minds who always seemed to find
that I never really would be quite enough.

On day three, I was the villain of my dreams.
Tied up in a bow with a noose made of long hair –
Silly little rabbit in a self-made snare.
Life on the other side isn't what it seems;
Silly little rabbits shouldn't scheme.

On the fourth day, I fiddled with bowties,
Dresses on summer days,
And precisely three lies to make sure I made it from bed
    on time
because life does not wait for the right outfit.

When I could manage it,
I'd glitter up my man bits and prance about a bit
in hopes of a tip or a legitimate compliment
because this ego deflates faster than a blimp with like
    sixty holes.
And, in the game against myself, I'm sometimes not so
    successful.

Ah well.

Here we are, day five, certainly not my last.
Chin up to the future, I'll tip my hat to the past,
And in spite of all the lunacy that livens up my life,
I listen when my gut says go.

DANEWOODLAND

ADAGES I

There is an adage known as The Golden Rule, which states the following: "Do unto others as you would have them do unto you." As a person who was raised to accept this principle, it was a major influence on the way I interacted with others while moving through the early stages of my gender transition. When approached by others who were seeking advice related to the negative experiences we have with those who do not *understand* people like myself, I would confidently point to The Golden Rule as my guide. I would assert the fact that it was important to lead by example, and that I must be accepting if I wanted acceptance in return.

Now that I have had some experience employing this methodology, I can see how it has failed me, and many others, in a variety of ways. Although this approach seemed admirable at the time, it is far from what I want for myself and even further from what I want for our general understanding of how we should treat one another, regardless of gender.

I first began to recognize the flaws in my approach when I attended a feminist event at a local student-union bar. The speaker pointed out something I had never really considered, which is that The Golden Rule is complete and utter bullshit. While it serves as a great model for kindness and respect for one another, it overlooks the fact that it is made on the basis of assumption. What I mean is that "doing onto others as you would have them do unto you" assumes that what is good for you, is good for someone else. Given that the world is full of so many wonderful, diverse, and unique individuals who all have different needs for comfort, safety, and contentment, isn't it a little silly to assume that what makes me happy would be the key to happiness for someone else? I think that it is—and that's how I shot myself in the foot while trying to get others to accept me as a transgender person.

ADAGES II

There is another adage—this one says that we teach others the way that we would like to be treated. *This* is something I have hung onto while trying to examine the way I interact with others. I have come to understand that I am responsible for the surroundings in which I place myself, the persons with whom I interact, and the behaviours that I deem acceptable. In the time that I was desperately seeking validation and comfort from those who questioned my gender identity and everything that came with it, I chose to not only tolerate, but accept their harmful attitudes and actions, in hopes that leading by example would eventually guide them to a place where they tolerated and accepted me. As these sorts of interactions continued to occur, I felt my discontentment lingering. I despaired because I was moving forward with my gender transition, feeling more comfortable and confident within myself, but perplexed because I was still so distressed. Wasn't this supposed to make me happier? I often asked myself that question when I found myself, deeply burrowed in the rabbit hole, desperately clamouring for solutions to my problems. Finally, I realized that it was not the actions of others that were the problem, but my own actions; finally, I realized that I was teaching people what was and wasn't acceptable behaviour.

It wasn't until I experienced a traumatic relationship that I came to realize how much my insecurity caused me to endure mistreatment. I allowed myself to undergo numerous harmful experiences, much to the horror of my friends and family, simply because this person had made me feel comfortable as a transgender man. This was the first person who had *not* emphasized the fact that I was trans. This person routinely expressed that "a person is a person is a person," and I clung to those words so tightly that I seemingly lost my grip on everything else. When things started to go wrong, I couldn't stand the loss of what I had built up to be the ultimate romantic relationship. I did everything in my power to try and keep things afloat—I sacrificed my goals, my values, and more than anything else, I sacrificed my entire sense of self. I was willing to give up anything if it meant that I could continue to be with someone who just saw me as a plain old *guy*, and not as a transgender person, or a person with mismatched body parts, or a person who was born female, or as anything other than what I wanted to be, which was just a plain old guy. While pursuing this ideal of the quintessential, everyday dude, what I ended up becoming was a version of myself that I hope to never see again. While that experience was awful in many ways, I think it was the "rock bottom" that I needed because it showed me what could happen when I left the determination of my sense of self up to someone else. Isn't that a little counterintuitive? I was willing to challenge biology, my family, my peers, my society all in an effort to establish myself as who I thought I was, but then relinquished my control on other parts of my identity just to ensure that the other piece—my gender—was accepted.

Acceptance isn't what I want, and neither is tolerance. What I want, for both myself and others, is understanding. Just as I would hope to understand others, I would hope that they would understand me. If they don't, I have no place for them.

Let me repeat that. If someone cannot have understanding for me, I have no place for them in my life. Conversely, I don't think I have much of a place in the life of someone for whom I lack understanding. If I am to treat someone the way that they would like to be treated, shouldn't I understand? How can I make them happy if I don't? How can you make me happy if you don't truly understand me? How could I make myself happy without truly understanding myself?

ADAGES III

This is where I have arrived, and am I ever glad that I've come to this point. Understanding myself has been a hard-fought battle, and it is, and forever will be, ongoing, but I am confident that I am developing and bettering the skills that I need. I don't venture down that rabbit hole quite so often anymore—I have not wondered whether my gender transition was supposed to make me happy. Instead, I am confident that it has. More than that, I am confident that *I* have made myself happy. By making my happiness about my gender identity, I made *everything* about my gender identity because my happiness *is* everything to me. That is why I was willing to go through all of this in the first place, after all. I did it because I wanted to be happy, and I can proudly say that I am. Now that I have realized that, I am willing to do whatever it takes to preserve that happiness.

Here is where those adages kick in: You teach others the ways that you would like to be treated. Remember what I said about people having a place in my life? If they don't treat me the way I'd like to be treated, my old methodology of leading by example is useless. Why would I ever tolerate something like that, especially when tolerance is far from my overall goal? The more that I have had the willingness to remove myself from harmful persons and environments, the happier I have been. Seems easy, right? Wrong. It's not; it's actually really hard. But it is worth it. In that same vein, this whole idea of being seen as a person rather than being seen as a *trans* person is my doing, as well. The more I emphasize it, the more it will be emphasized by others. The more I make it the source of both my happiness and my sadness, the more that it *will* be the source of my happiness and sadness. I have spent way too much time trying to decide whether an issue has been because I am trans or because I am a person, and I realize how problematic that sort of attitude is. The reality is that all people face struggles. The context within which those struggles exists is very different based from one person to the next, but the bottom line is the same: to struggle is to be human. I am privileged in some ways, yet I am disadvantaged in others—while I work to maintain a steady gaze on this reality, I must remind myself of who I am. I am, first and foremost, a person, and that identity of personhood is what unites me with everyone around me. That identity of personhood is what helps me to find relatability, avoid isolation, and establish and maintain a place of belonging. That identity of personhood is what keeps me grounded when I am woeful about my experience as a trans person and how my gender identity shapes me. The way that I navigate my time on earth is up to me. So, no, I won't treat others the way that I want to be treated, because I have enough trouble figuring out what I want, let alone figuring out what others want. Instead of assuming, I will ask, and I will observe. I will seek and accept feedback, and I will continually strive to improve. *This* is the sort of leading by example that I *would* like to employ. Not by demonstrating my acceptance of harmful attitudes, but by demonstrating my desire to know and understand so that I may act appropriately. If someone is not willing to do the same for me, they do not have a place in my life, and that's totally fine because their absence will make space for someone who *is* willing to do the same for me. I make this commitment not as a trans person, but as a person, which doesn't make me all that different from anyone else, which is exactly how I'd like to be seen.

FASCINATION

What is this fascination
With the bodies of people
Who are trans

You look at us like
We are car crashes
Or train wrecks
Wanting to look away
But maintaining a steady gaze

You erase the essence
Of what makes us human
Separating our bodies
From our souls
Separating our parts
From our bodies

When I hear
'What an amazing transformation'
I can't help but wonder
If you give the same notice
To the changes *every* body undergoes
The more we experience
The more we grow

You may think that we change
Differently than you
But do you know anyone
Who has changed
In the same way as you?

When I read
'Top ten guys you won't believe
Were born female'
I can't help but wonder
If you are celebrating
Or gawking
And snickering
As you sheepishly consider
That you may find someone like me
Attractive
But could never imagine
Touching them
Knowing them
Or loving them

When I think
Trans folks are making progress
I am sobered by the thought
That we are mostly visible
Because of our bodies
Seen because we
'Don't look trans'
Or, because we do.

And while this is hurtful as hell
We fall in line
And play with the hand we've been dealt
In hopes that our words will
Not just be heard, but felt.

Are you listening now?

TRANSVERSING

transVersing was first produced by Artistic Fraud and For The Love Of Learning on March 28, 2017, at the Barbara Barrett Theatre in St. John's, NL. It featured the following cast and creative team:

Writers/Performers: Violet Drake, Daze Jefferies, Fionn Shea, Perin Squires, Taylor Stocks, and Dane Woodland

Director/Dramaturge: Berni Stapleton

Assistant Director/Dramaturge: Sharon King-Campbell

Video Editor: Robert Chafe

Stage Manager: Sharon King-Campbell

For the Barbara Barrett Theatre: Dale Drew

The play's first professional main-stage debut occurred in September of 2017, for the St. John's Short Play Festival, at the LSPU Hall, featuring the following cast and creative team:

Writer/Performers: Violet Drake, Fionn Shea, Taylor Stocks, Dane Woodland

Director/Dramaturge: Berni Stapleton

Assistant Director/Dramaturge: Sharon King-Campbell

Stage Manager: Crystal Lafolley

For the Short Play Festival TD: Mara Bredovskis

For the LSPU Hall: Patrick Dempsey and Robert Gauthier

This version of the script of *transVersing* is meant to be adaptable to varying sizes of cast. Although all of the originating cast of the workshop presentation could not participate in the theatre version of this script, monologues from the anthology may be added to the stage version.

Fionn's monologue in the finale of the show is from Shakespeare's *King Lear*, Edmund's monologue from Act One, Scene Two. In order to be inclusive of as many contributors as possible, some monologues, as seen in the anthology portion of this book, were recorded and have been used as video components of the play.

We encourage performers to bring their own musical explorations to their productions. Our performers used a range of instruments including synthesizers, guitar, trombone, and percussion. Any forms of dance or movement are welcome.

transVersing

Four chairs are on the stage in a slight semi-circle. Any musical instruments or props needed for the performance are present on the stage, on stands or hung on the chairs. The stage is lit.

Houselights go down. The performers walk on stage, each person standing in front of their chair. They take a full moment to look at each other before looking at the audience. Throughout the play, the performers will stay engaged with each other, exchanging looks and encouragement between transitions.

     VIOLET
In my youth I found solace within a book more
     than anywhere.
Ink never screamed, nor did paper ever hit.

     TAYLOR
Before I was born, I ran away,
I had whispers of the wrong words, of what I
     couldn't say.

VIOLET
Stories have always fascinated, and
     fashioned me.
Be about masks, dummies, and vampires,
Or lions, witches, and wardrobes,
pages bound together could always be found
     between my palms.

TAYLOR
When I saw a shadow of myself, I hid
in the promise of perfection, precious
     womanhood
and I screamed when my gut said no
drowning out the doubts
but I wouldn't be the same
cuz I couldn't quite escape
that perhaps I wanted out.

FIONN
I dare you to look at my body and tell me I am
     deformed.

DANE
What is this fascination with the bodies of people
     who are Trans?

FIONN
I dare you to look at me and tell me I don't exist.

DANE
You look at us like we're car crashes.

VIOLET

The book was my umbrella during the storms of
     my peers,
 a sanctuary only my eye could see
where my *I* was at peace.
A place where I/eye could be anywhere else.

FIONN

I dare you to look at me and tell me I am not
     enough.

VIOLET

Beyond the four walls of brick and cement,
pristine and ivory:
matching the armour across my face.

TAYLOR

On day one, I heard a wilted echo
sitting round the circle, watching as the mouths bled
breathing every beat, feeding what didn't know
So I painted him, and he came alive
standing in the mirror, looking at me through my
     eyes.
I couldn't feel my chest for the chafing of the tape
But here he was, of me, in him, for me to realize.

FIONN

I fucking hate chest binders. They save my life
every day and I despise them. My pages fold into
them, pages of a story I'd really rather forget.

DANE

You want to look away but maintain a steady gaze.
You erase the essence of what makes us human,
separating our bodies from our souls, separating
our parts from our bodies.

VIOLET

I'd watch the other boys from here,
all those who were outside the main text:
one that we all learned from the Jersey Room to
    Sandy Point.
The same text that left me illegible to those that
    birthed me.

TAYLOR

On the second day I clung to the breeze
desperate for the company that comes from being she
I swore I'd make room in those words
it was never my intention to give them to the birds
but I just couldn't find my verse
even up on stage, I was plagued by the girl curse
damning petty little minds who always seemed to find
that I never really would be quite enough.

FIONN

Pages I'd like nothing better to forget, rip from my
body. With a binder I am able to forget they exist
until I have trouble breathing because my fucking
ten hours are up and off it comes.

Or doesn't.

DANE

When I hear "what an amazing transformation" I
can't help but wonder if you give the same notice
to the changes *every* body undergoes, the more
we experience, the more we grow.

VIOLET

Where I come from, gender is thought to be
    intransient;
a dichotomous stone mirroring the underbelly of
    this island.
Still, I breathe and weave a *you and me*.
I reside on this rock just as you and the rest of
    us do.

TAYLOR

On day three I was the villain of my dreams
tied up in a bow with a noose made out of long
    hair
silly little rabbit in a self-made snare
life on the other side isn't what it seems
silly little rabbits shouldn't scheme

FIONN

Sweet relief, accompanied by dysphoria. I forget
that people are heartbroken by the pain I cause
myself to live. Let me remind you that a lack of
breath is not a lack of life, but a love of living.

I dare you.

DANE

You may think we change differently than you,
but do you know anyone who has changed in the
same way as you?

VIOLET

I too have had my fair share of tickets from the
        gender police,
and trips to Manning's Beach.
When my school crest changed from burgundy to blue,
I graduated from HNMA,
yet never enrolled into manhood.

TAYLOR

On the fourth day, I fiddled with bowties
dresses on summer days and precisely three lies
to make sure I made it from bed on time
because life doesn't wait for the right outfit.

FIONN

Look past my tension and past my scars. See the
scars that come from years of bra shopping and
getting makeup for a birthday because "Every girl
should have makeup."

DANE

When I read "top ten guys you won't believe were
born female," I can't help but wonder if you are
celebrating or gawking and snickering as you
sheepishly consider that you may find someone
like me attractive.

VIOLET

My first winter as a university student
had me read both fiction and fact;
through both I grew my voice.
This marked the first time that the word
    transgender
welcomed me in school.
 It was in my very first dorm
where the same palms that held the shield of my
    younger self
crafted me a key instead.

TAYLOR

When I could manage it,
I'd glitter up my man bits and prance about a bit
in hopes of a tip or a legitimate compliment
because this ego deflates faster than a blimp with
    like sixty holes.
And in the game against myself, I'm sometimes
    not so successful.
Ah well.

FIONN

See me as more than a body, as more than a
shape, as more than the things we use to bind
ourselves together, like a corpse with its jaws tied.

I dare you, I dare you, I dare you.

DANE

Could you ever imagine touching me, knowing
me, or loving me? We are visible because of our
bodies, seen because we "don't look" trans, or
because we do.

VIOLET

The key to a place far greater than the imaginary,
more dangerous than Narnia,
and certainly more magical than Hogwarts.
It's 2012 and I am in the backseat of my parent's
     trusted minivan
where I disclose in between their screams:
"I'm transgender."

EACH PERSON REPEATS
     (quietly)
I'm transgender.

VIOLET

My mother replies: *"You just think you are the next
     thing you read in your books."*
I can't help but wonder
how different all this would be
if she too were a bookworm.

TAYLOR

Now day five, certainly not my last
chin up to the future, I'll tip my hat to the past
And in spite of all the lunacy that livens up my
     life
I listen when my gut says go.

FIONN

And I bind myself together day after day after day after day after day. I bind myself to this world because I remember what it's like to breathe clearly. So I dare you.

DANE

We fall in line and play with the hand we've been dealt, in hope that our words will not just be heard, but felt.

Are you listening now?

FIONN

I dare you. I dare you. I dare you.

ALL

(slowly, not in unison, repeating the refrain until Taylor is ready to sing.)
I dare you. I dare you. I dare you. I dare you.

Everyone sits except for Taylor and Fionn. Accompaniment for the song was provided by Fionn on percussion. Fionn also did harmony.

TAYLOR

My boyfriend left me yesterday
He told me girl you are too queer
I said I don't know what you're saying
There ain't no woman standing here.

[chorus]
I'm a transient twister, an elegant mister
A boy big sister with a cock
My gender it flows cuz that's how it goes
Living trans life out on the rock
I sparkle and glow so all of you know
I'm living trans life out on the rock
Woke up today feeling kind of lazy
I didn't want to have to work it giiiiirl
Something in my head was driving me right crazy
Felt like it was me against the world
What do you do when your chest betrays you
Your best assets make you feel like a fool

[chorus]
I'm a transient twister, an elegant mister
A boy big sister with a cock
My gender it flows cuz that's how it goes
Living trans life out on the rock
I sparkle and glow so all of you know
I'm living trans life out on the rock

[bridge]
I want you to know that being she makes me feel
    queasy
I want you to know that the men of the world
    won't let me be he
I want you to know that the woman inside of me is
    still alive and
I want you to know I want you to know...

[chorus]
I'm a transient twister, an elegant mister
A boy big sister with a cock
My gender it flows cuz that's how it goes
Living trans life out on the rock
I sparkle and glow so all of you know
I'm living trans life out on the rock.

Taylor sits. Dane stands.

DANE

Do unto others as you would have them do unto
you. That's The Golden Rule. It was a major
influence on the way I interacted with others
through the early stages of my gender transition.

When I was approached by others who
were seeking advice related to the negative
experiences we have with those who do
not *understand* people like myself, I would
confidently point to The Golden Rule as my
guide. I would assert the fact that it was important
to lead by example, and that I must be accepting
if I wanted acceptance in return.

The Golden Rule is bullshit.

It's failed me in a variety of ways. Although this
approach seemed admirable at the time, it's far
from what I want for myself and even further from
what I want for our general understanding of how
we should treat one another, regardless of gender.

It serves as a great model for kindness and respect for one another, but it is made on the basis of assumption. "Doing onto others as you would have them do unto you" assumes that what is good for you, is good for someone else.

The world is full of so many wonderful, diverse, and unique individuals who all have different needs for comfort, safety, and contentment, it's silly to assume that what makes me happy would be the key to happiness for someone else.

That's how I shot myself in the foot while trying to get others to accept me as a transgender person.

Dane gets his trombone as Fionn stands.

FIONN
I am a bastard child of the so-called American dream and American identity.

Dane plays a line from Simon and Garfunkle's "America," then sits.

FIONN
I am a bastard child because I was born into a body that refuses to conform, a mind that refuses the binary, and a soul that refuses a black-and-white identity. I am a bastard child because I was born into a society that refuses my manhood, that forces my womanhood, and that knocks me down while telling me to pick myself up by the

bootstraps. Because that's the American dream—work hard and you'll succeed.

Well I've worked hard. And damn if I won't succeed.

I am a bastard child in my identity, but also in my age. Like my country, I am young. And when we're young, we expend so much time and so much creative energy into trying to hide who we really are, trying to change things that people made fun of—"your voice is too high, your stature is too small, but you're legitimate! You're just not enough."

I am a bastard child of America, but I've learned from those that have come before me. I've learned that our existences are not a mistake, that we are not invisible. This is something to shout from the rooftops when they send the dogs after us, it is something to sing in the streets even when we are blocked by white supremacists and state senators, it is something to be played in the theater, even when the crowds have all gone home, it is the thing that we must bring to light to save our lives and our communities from the trap of fear that is the unknown.

For the boy who cannot come out for fear his parents will disown him, for the girl who is told she is invisible in the school halls and in the senate halls, I have one message: we hear you, we will hold your hand; we must stay together,

no matter what our gender, no matter what our
skin colour, no matter if we're born here (like you,
like me) or immigrants (like me, like you). We've
been down this road before, we, the young, the
old, the strong, the hungry: we know hatred. We
know bigotry. We know fear. We do not have the
privilege of sitting quiet while our family dies,
not when walking out your front door is an act
of rebellion and every breath resonates like a
gunshot—until we die or it changes, keep fighting.

I am a self-made American bastard. And I plan to
stay that way.

*Dane stands and plays the same line on the trombone. They
both sit. Violet stands.*

VIOLET
On the cusp of
adolescence
is when I found
virtue without virtus

September 8th, 2010:
otherwise known as
the anniversary of
myself and makeup

Each time this month
sprouted on the calendar
I was greeted with
a ripe new grade

By the time that my
front lawn turned lush
the beauty bug had
already infected me

Whereas most boys my
age spent their summer
fulfilling their father's hunting pacts,
I made my own with the mirror

They set snares
as I set powder,
both of us bonded
in execution

My trophy animal
found not in trees
but between selves;
the rhizome of envy

Crisp lines of slate
across the eyelid,
or architecture of
an alabastrine complexion

Detoxifying my eyes
I unearth myself,
becoming chimera:
hybrid, implausible, absurd

Encased inside
four navy walls
is where I committed
my first murder

The amalgamation
of rigour and diligence;
a crime traced in
kohl and rouge

Bade adieu to qualms
with each stroke
forging me anew;
facere vera

Apostle androgyne
through osmosis is
heir to a new faith,
catharsis sans Catholicism

I begin to grow akin
to the power of glass
reap what I sow
on uncharted terrain

Bearing witness
to none but me
I make my initial molt,
the onset of my haunting

When my eyes met hers
for the very first time
a glimpse of home
was found to be mine

The imagined made real
shot adrenaline through
every stem of me;
gendersynthesis

Visceral now victorious,
a new epistemology
is born; situated
against the grain

Drunk on pride,
my newfound wings
glide me down the hall
to my father's dwelling place

Wide eyed and bright
I showcase the fruit
of my labour, to which he responds:
"what have you got done to yourself, my son?"

The gloss in my eye dimmed
and toward the hall I ran,
flesh seared in scorn
and blood boiled in shame

Magic mutated into monstrosity,
I crawl back into my cave
vowing never to let another
burn me for my beauty again.

Violet sits as Taylor stands.

> TAYLOR

There are rainbows in my chest
swirling, in the cavern of my ribcage
Bright colours, though dark ones too
Ever changing,
constant movement
within a static frame.

And who doesn't want a heart full of rainbows?
The delightfulness of such simple coloured
pleasure as an added topping upon daily
drudgery—it seems a gift to have such a spectacle
so close to my lungs

For each one of my breaths is filled with rich hues
vibrantly mixed with the next and next until my
throat is charged with multicoloured text. Words
filled with wisdom of what it is to move with a
force of nature.

But,
Sometimes they make me sick
An oily gasoline sheen sticking between my ribs
Yet too slippery to grip It makes me queasy

The shifting and lilting
my stomach can't keep up with the ragged
rhythms tossed about in a storm that can't
decide if it is fundamentally more aligned with
the inherent internal properties of red or blue
Philosophy is no life boat.

There are no answers,
few words that allow communication across
the tempest And sometimes it takes too much
To figure out what it takes to be seen when
alignment is a laughable construction.

There isn't, then,
Much else to be done
Except to move too
And enjoy the pretty colours as they come.

Taylor sits as Dane stands.

> DANE
> There is another old adage: we teach others the
> way that we would like to be treated. *This* is one
> I've hung onto.
>
> I'm responsible for the surroundings in which
> I place myself, the people I interact with, the
> behaviour I deem acceptable. In the time
> that I was desperately seeking validation and
> comfort from those who questioned my gender
> identity, I chose to tolerate their harmful
> attitudes and actions, in hopes that leading by

example would eventually mean they would tolerate and accept me.

I felt my discontentment.

I despaired.

I was moving forward with my gender transition, feeling more comfortable and confident within myself, but I was still so distressed.

Wasn't this supposed to make me happier?

I found myself deeply burrowed in the rabbit hole, desperately clamouring for solutions to my problems.

I sacrificed my goals, my values, I sacrificed my entire sense of self. I was willing to give up anything if it meant that I could be seen as a plain old *guy*, and not as a transgender person, or a person with mismatched body parts, or a person who was born female, or as anything other than what I wanted to be.

A plain old guy.

I ended up becoming a version of myself that I hope to never see again.

It was the "rock bottom" that I needed, because it showed me what could happen when I left

the determination of my sense of self up to
someone else.

Acceptance isn't what I want, and neither is
tolerance. What I want is understanding. I would
hope to understand others. I hope others will
understand me.
How can you make me happy if you don't truly
understand me? How could I make myself happy
without truly understanding myself?

Dane sits as Fionn stands.

> FIONN
> You tight-lipped, silver-tongued, Goddess-
>   worshipping, moonlight baby, snowfall
>   huntress,
> You were born into blood and born to the
>   bleeding,
> the cord wrapped thrice around your neck
> the noose you wouldn't wear in life was formed by
>   your life itself
> Backwards, upside-down, crying, you came into
>   the world screaming heathen rites, blood
>   boiling in the
> midwife's veins and she thought you a fairy child
> blood ritual anointed your birth
> your mother knew that soon you would begin to
>   bleed
> You strong, fierce, tender-hearted, sharp-minded
>   hunter

You were built and put together from pieces taken
     out of the body of your Mother
any gender can bleed
a learned skill from blood mother and blood
     father
Changeling-child, river-driver, quick-footed,
     wordsmith, dragon
The sac that once held you gave way to your own
     walls, the umbilical cord severed but the link
     held fast
your blood flows with the moon rites
boys can bleed too.

Fionn sits as Taylor stands.

TAYLOR

Dear Mum,

Help me craft this middle space. Help me
building a wreckhouse place where the winds of
the world would rather I not be.

Help me define sanity against the lines placed by
small minds. Help me divine an etcetera of many
kinds of wishes and wants unconfined by boxes
too stiff for any of us to live.

Come with me. Come follow me to a rainbow bliss
that is all at once everything and freedom from
what is. Come with me and see the magic that is
movement within places that won't bend us out of
shape just to brighten faces of those we love.

Come see what I've made, what I've paid dearly
for: a breath that doesn't have to land between the
beats of two and four, something more than the
tragic defeat of our inner souls as we meet our
fate just outside the door...

I want to show you where I dance. Where, in a dress
or pants, I gallivant across the floor. Where sequins
and sparkles bedazzle my prancing and I'm
dancing, dancing, and maybe there's safety near...

I want to show you where my heart sings. Where,
in ribbons and things, my song rings clearer than
this smoky voice could ever manage here...

It's silly to put such stock in a house dressed
of pronouns and nicknames, word games and
mountains of clumsy language. But it wasn't
the tip that hit the ship and my buoyancy is
dependent on my boyness, see?

And even though it feels like a betrayal to eschew
phrases of girl that brought you and me to the
same basis of being, I've made this place anyway
and I'd like you to visit often and have a T that
isn't quite so steeped in woman. I find she's less
bitter.

I'm seeing more than I ever thought I could
before and yes, it's my pain that's brought me
here, but I've found so many colours to paint with
that I don't fear the darkness eating through my

core. Sure I can't erase historic lore, but I can stick with it and craft my story into a mythic life raft that can lift me when I can't swim anymore.

You've given me wit and wonder and I want to bring you to my distant shore where the sun is bright but doesn't burn and the patterns of patriarchy have had their turn and are content to sit idly by, unsurprisingly fine, half-toasted on expensive wine.

Yet that's not quite it. I don't know how to describe this vague explicit notion that seems only to exist in my mind...(except, of course, on Fridays, when I actually buy this gist of this fifty horse power thought binge)...Most days I can't help but cringe that I'm host to a plurality that the world around me says is a fib. But when my inside bells chime in perfectly syncopated time, I'm captured by the rhythm and I'm dancing, dancing...

Oh please, dear Mummy, come and dance with me. You've given me everything, at least I can give you this: my third space of love and creation, a new patience for change, and a fierce determination to stay in a moving place. I give you my rhyme to share what is, and forever my love, which will remain always, one plus infinite.

And my mother opened her arms wide and her
heart wider and put on her dancing shoes…

And said *yes*, my precious one. Take me there.

*Taylor dances accompanied by Fionn on the fiddle. The
dance ends and Taylor sits, but Fionn continues to play for a
while until the song is over.*

*Everyone stands for the finale. Taylor sings and plays
guitar. The song is mingled with spoken word, as indicated
in the text.*

> TAYLOR
> *(sings)*
> I don't know how to be a boy
> to grow up and have man as my choice
> to grow old with a baritone voice
> I don't know how to be a boy
>
> I don't know how to be a girl
> to grow up and be a woman in the world
> to grow old as my lady unfurls
> I don't know how to be a girl

Instrumentation continues underneath as Dane speaks.

> DANE
> This is where I have arrived.

Understanding myself has been a hard-fought
battle.

It is and forever will be ongoing.

I don't venture down that rabbit hole quite so often anymore.

I haven't wondered whether my gender transition has made me happy. I'm confident that it has.

I have made myself happy.

By making my happiness about my gender identity, I made everything about my gender identity. That's why I was willing to go through all of this in the first place. I did it because I want to be happy. I'm willing to do whatever it takes it preserve this happiness.

The more I have the willingness to remove myself from harmful persons and environments, the happier I am. Seems easy, right? It's actually really hard. This whole idea of being seen as a person rather than being seen as a *trans* person, well, the more I emphasize it, the more it will be emphasized by others. The more I make it the source of my happiness and my sadness, the more that it *will* be the source of my happiness and sadness. I've spent way too much time trying to decide whether a problem is because I'm trans or because I am a person.

All people face struggles. That makes us who we are: to struggle is to be human.

I work to maintain a steady gaze on this reality, to remind myself of who I am.

A person. The identity of personhood is what unites me with everyone around me.

The way that I navigate my time on earth is up to me. I won't treat others the way that I want to be treated, I've got enough trouble figuring out what I want, let alone figuring out what others want.

Instead of assuming, I'll ask, and I'll observe. I'll seek and accept feedback, I continually strive to improve. *This* is the sort of leading by example that I like to employ.

I make this commitment not as a trans person, but as a person with diverse layers of needs that have been shaped by my experiences thus far. Doesn't make me all that different from anyone else.

      TAYLOR
   (sings)
Now I gotta ask
What the hell do you know of that
From where I'm sitting
It's not as if you've got a good definition
Maybe it's true
I'm not so different from you
Well how about that

I don't know how to be a femme
To save myself from being consumed by men
To grow old and not take shit from them
I don't know how to be a femme

Instrumentation continues underneath as Violet speaks.

VIOLET

I wander around this world every day
yet I go completely unseen
my gender is ectoplasm,
just a trace left by a phantom like me

What does it mean to be a ghost,
a being trapped between this world and the
    afterlife
is there even a life after one such as this:
a life of translucency, indecency, and strife

My identity is often transparent and lost,
at best dislocated, dismembered, or disavowed
most think I am found in the blackness that
    frames my eyes
yet in the heart of every dead boy is where I reside

Eyes and lips,
stares and glares
caught between distain and desire,
pass through me as if I am nothing but
    nothingness itself

I am the air that is inhaled during your gasps,
the carbon dioxide released from your exhale
the glue that keeps everything together:
taken for granted and unseen

We are often deceived by the sparkle of visibility
"Recognition fuels volition" a queer activist says
     to me,
how many women like me have died chasing that
     rabbit
down the hole that leads her to Venus
     Extravaganza's wonderland

A girl like me is not unusual yet often made a
     spectacle,
who better to know the high price of being a muse
to cross genders is carnivalesque, suspension in
     transition
truth mutated into transgression

My trace is found in the racing heart of women
     like me walking home at night
the ways in which our bodies and genders are
     defined and confined,
policed and disposed of for the threat of resisting
     order
I wish my sister Leelah Alcorn could have grew
     older

My pulse is felt in every
"Sorry, I'm not used to this"
"What exactly are you," and
"I didn't mean to be offensive, you know what I
mean though"

I'm bruised by all the
"I'm just not into that,"
"So really you are a man," or
"You'll find someone right for you someday"

Always exhausted of the unfairness in
"But I'm the one who gave birth to you,"
"You've deceived me for so long," and
"Then why bother doing this if it's this hard"

Constantly plagued by the uncertainty of
"Am I going to come home tonight,"
"Will I ever feel okay in the skin I am in," or
"Who will ever love me if I tell the truth?"

Who attains to me in my time of need,
to soak my wounds and nourish my soul
when my shoulders get weak
everyone in this city is travelling in one way or
another
but how many apparitions like me are stuck in limbo

What creatures of this island
are part of my clan of vampires
can't find themselves in the hanging glass,
left with stomachs full of thorns

Monsters that blend vitality and fatality,
augment the organic with the artificial
all with a taste for the same invigorating blood:
an antidote for dysphoria.

TAYLOR
(sings)
I don't know how to be man
To take up space cuz they all say I can
To hold the world in the palm of my hand
I don't know how to be a man

Instrumentation continues underneath as Fionn speaks.

FIONN
Thou, Nature, art my goddess; to thy law
My services are bound. Wherefore should I
Stand in the plague of custom, and permit
The curiosity of nations to deprive me,
For that I am some twelve or fourteen moonshines
Lag of a brother? Why bastard? Wherefore base?
When my dimensions are as well compact,
My mind as generous, and my shape as true,
As honest madam's issue? Why brand they us
With base? with baseness? bastardy? base, base?
Who, in the lusty stealth of nature, take
More composition and fierce quality
Than doth within a dull, stale, tired bed
Go about creating a whole tribe of fops
Got b'tween sleep and wake
Well then, legitimate Edgar, I must have your
    land.

Our father's love is to the bastard Edmund
As to th' legitimate. Fine word—'legitimate'!
Well, my legitimate, if this letter speed,
And my invention thrive, Edmund the base
Shall top th' legitimate. I grow; I prosper.
Now, gods, stand up for bastards!

TAYLOR
        (sings)
So you know I gotta ask
What the hell do you know of that
From where I'm sitting
It's not as if you've got a good definition
Maybe it's true
I'm not so different from you
Well how about that

I know how to be me
Turns out I don't mind my own company
When I'm myself, I am truly free
I know how to be me.

The end. Cast bow. Lights down.

Artistic Fraud of Newfoundland would like to acknowledge the funding support of the following: Arts NL, Canada Council for the Arts, the City of St. John's, and Canada 150 (Department of Canadian Heritage).

For the Love of Learning would like to acknowledge the Government of NL.

CONTRIBUTORS

Violet Drake is a poet, visual artist, and activist born and raised in the small coastal community of Lawn, Newfoundland. Now based in St. John's, her work explores queer and trans intimacies, embodied trauma, and place-based poetics. She has engaged with academic, artistic, and activist audiences through conferences, workshops, speeches, and performances. She is currently finishing her debut poetry collection *estrogenesis*.

Daze Jefferies is a multidisciplinary artist, poet, and researcher at Memorial University with interests in trans health, sex work, queer archives, and emotional geographies. Her ongoing critical-creative work explores trans-species (fishy) histories, poetics, and subjectivities in K'taqamkuk/Newfoundland. She is co-author of *Autoethnography and Feminist Theory at the Water's Edge: Unsettled Islands* (Palgrave Pivot 2018).

Sharon King-Campbell is a writer, storyteller, and theatre artist based in St. John's. She has been working in the theatre for more than a decade as a performer, director, producer, and playwright. Sharon is the author of two plays, *Fighting Fire with Snow* (World's End Theatre Company) and *Give Me Back* (skc originals/For the Love of Learning). She is the artistic director of skc originals, and is pursuing her Master's in English at Memorial University.

Fionn Shea is an actor, activist, musician, and writer from New Hampshire. Their background in the arts is varied. Shakespearian theatre, New England contra dance music, and house-training a baby lamb have all been in the mix. Fionn's writing has appeared on New Hampshire Public Radio and in the *Concord Monitor*, and they have worked for organizations such as the American Civil Liberties Union of New Hampshire and the National Abortion Rights Action League. Fionn is an habitual tea-drinker, a huge *Hamilton* geek, and a marketing assistant for Blasty Bough Brewing Company, in that order. At age twelve they were the youngest person ever awarded a state-sponsored apprenticeship to study traditional music, and in the same year, covered the Democratic National Convention for a national youth magazine—their biggest accomplishments so far, however, are knowing how to operate a rototiller and make maple syrup. Fionn is currently completing a BA Honours degree in English at Memorial University of Newfoundland.

Perin Squires is a gender-queer artist who currently lives in London, Ontario. They grew up by the ocean in Port au Port, Newfoundland, and is currently working on a BA in theatre, a major in English, a minor in Film Studies, and a diploma in Performance and Media Communications.

Berni Stapleton is a Newfoundland and Labrador writer and performer of unique distinction. She has received the 2018 Arts and Letters award for best dramatic script, The Rhonda Payne award from ArtsNL, the WANL award for best work in non-fiction for her contribution to *They Let Down Baskets*, and the Ambassador of Tourism Award from Hospitality NL. Her short stories and essays have appeared in *Riddle Fence* and the *Newfoundland Quarterly*. Berni was the Artistic Director of the Grand Bank Regional Theatre Festival for eleven years, and she has been a playwright-in-residence with the Stratford Shakespeare Festival, Playwrights' Workshop Montreal, Alberta Theatre Projects, CanStage, PARC, and other national companies. Her plays are regularly produced nationally and internationally. They include *Offensive to Some*, *Brazil Square*, *The Haunting of Margaret Duley*, and *Our Frances*. Berni's other books include *This is the Cat* and *Rants, Riffs and Roars*, and she is currently writing a young-adult novel entitled *Girly Muckle and the Queer Hands*. Her new one-woman show is called *Late Lesbians and Other Bloomers*, and she is one of the featured performers in the acclaimed Artistic Fraud production of *Between Breaths*. You can find out more about Berni and her work at bernistapleton.com.

Taylor Stocks is a genderfluid trans activist living in St. John's. Stocks is chair of the St. John's Inclusion Advisory Committee, a member of Memorial University's Employment Equity and Diversity Advisory Committee, a director of the Trans Needs Committee, and former co-chair of St. John's Pride. In addition to their activism, they also explore and challenge gender through entertaining and unique music, poetry, and drag performance. Since 2013, Stocks' drag persona, Doctor Androbox, has shaken the local drag scene in St. John's and was the second Drag King to win the annual Drag Idol competition, taking home the crown in 2017. Stocks is a strong advocate for inclusion and is a regular contributor to local education and fundraising events. Stocks is set to begin their PhD in Education in September 2018.

Dane Woodland is a full-time fitness professional and part-time volunteer in St. John's. Through all avenues of his lifestyle, Dane imparts his knowledge in hopes of sparking positive change. Whether he is working to correct movement patterns, coaching young track-and-field athletes, or sharing his voice on behalf of the trans community, Dane is invested in communicating meaningfully and effectively. Dane's involvement in *transVersing* has allowed him to diversify his interests and develop skills as an artist while allowing him to integrate with other likeminded folks who can appreciate his experiences. As an activist, Dane regularly shares his personal stories as a means of creating more awareness of gender diversity. He gave a Ted Talk in 2016 entitled, "One Lifetime, Two Perspectives: How Male Privilege Made Me A Feminist," and he has appeared at many sessions, conferences, and professional seminars related to his experience as a trans person. Dane's vision is that *transVersing* will encourage greater interest in learning and the emergence and recognition of our talented and wonderful community.